A N...
at
KoKo Bear's House

A Practical Parenting
Read-Together Book

Vicki Lansky

Illustrated by Jane Prince

BANTAM BOOKS
TORONTO · NEW YORK · LONDON · SYDNEY · AUCKLAND

A NEW BABY AT KOKO BEAR'S HOUSE
A Bantam Book / March 1987

ISBN 0-553-34373-4

Published simultaneously in the United States and Canada

Bantam Books are published by Bantam Books, Inc. Its trademark, consisting of the words "Bantam Books" and the portrayal of a rooster, is Registered in U.S. Patent and Trademark Office and in other countries. Marca Registrada. Bantam Books, Inc., 666 Fifth Avenue, New York, New York 10103.

PRINTED IN THE UNITED STATES OF AMERICA

WAK   0 9 8 7 6 5 4 3 2 1

Introduction

The arrival of a new baby at your house is a major event and one that will have a strong impact on your older child(ren). We all worry about how the older child will react and how we can help him or her adjust. This new baby will change the older child's position in the family and be a competitor for love and attention. Through all this, we must work to keep our child's self-esteem intact.

One way you can help is by letting your child know what to expect. With that in mind, this story of the arrival of a new baby in KoKo Bear's family will guide your child through the key stages of your pregnancy, delivery, and homecoming.

To help you make this a smooth transition, there are tips and suggestions for parents on every page. You can skim these silently while you and your child read about KoKo. For more detailed material and additional tips, you may wish to refer to my companion book, Practical Parenting WELCOMING YOUR SECOND BABY.

While it will be necessary to give your older child extra love and attention and to make time for your marital relationship, don't make the mistake of not taking care of that necessary and very important person—YOU!

Sincerely,

Vicki Lansky

One morning MaMa Bear has good news to share. "KoKo," she says, "there is going to be a new baby at our house."

"For me?" asks KoKo happily.

"The baby will be for all of us," says PaPa Bear.

"When will the baby come?" asks KoKo.

MaMa Bear smiles and says, "Our new baby will be born when the flowers are blooming again, KoKo."

- *Don't introduce the idea of a new baby too soon if your child is very young. Nine months can be too long to understand. Save most of your preparations for closer to your due date.*
- *Speak of the baby as "ours," not as "mine" or your child's.*
- *Tie your due date to an event rather than a month. "After Christmas," or "when the snow disappears" are easier concepts for a child to understand.*

As the new baby grows inside MaMa Bear, she gets bigger and bigger.

"KoKo, when you hug me, you are also hugging our new baby," says MaMa. "I love your hugs, and I think the baby loves your hugs, too."

"Is our new baby a boy or a girl?" asks KoKo.

"We won't know that until the baby is born," answers MaMa Bear.

- *Explain pregnancy's physical changes in simple language. Long, detailed explanations aren't necessarily of interest to children.*
- *Talk about the new baby without emphasizing all the family changes that will take place, so the older child won't worry about being displaced.*
- *Stress that the gender of the unborn baby will be a surprise. Of course, if you know, that's a different matter.*

"**K**oKo, I have a new book to read to you," says PaPa Bear. "It's a story about how baby bears are born."

KoKo climbs onto PaPa's lap to see the pictures. "Can we read *Goldilocks and the Three Chairs,* too?" asks KoKo.

"Sure," says PaPa, "we'll read them both."

- *Pregnancy is a wonderful opportunity to teach reproductive information. Books exist for every age with explanations that vary from the poetic to the exact.*
- *Make any major changes, such as moving the child to a big bed or completing toilet training, well before the expected birth. Or wait until several months after the birth.*
- *"Borrow" a baby to babysit so your child will see how babies act and how much care they need.*

MaMa Bear and KoKo like looking at the family photo album.

KoKo points to a picture of a baby bear and asks, "Is that me?"

"Yes. And you're wearing the red hat that Aunt Beartrice knitted for you," says MaMa. "And this is the bear-pack we'll use for our new baby. You're too big for it now. Now you're my big grown-up bear."

- *Look at infant pictures with your child as a reminder of the attention he or she received as a baby.*
- *Use extra baby photos to make a child his or her very own photo album. Or together create a cut-and-paste scrapbook of baby pictures from magazines.*
- *Point out the many advantages of being older and more grown up. Praise any and all mature behavior you can spot in your child.*

"Today," MaMa says to KoKo, "we are going to have lunch at Honey Comb Hospital. That is where you were born. Our new baby will be born there, too."

"Will I come with you to the hospital?" asks KoKo.

"Today, yes, but not when it's time for our baby to be born. Penny Panda, your sitter, will stay with you at home," answers MaMa Bear.

- *Take your child to visit the hospital you'll be using. Have lunch in the cafeteria or just visit the gift shop. This makes the hospital a real place, not just an abstract—and somewhat scary—idea.*
- *Check your hospital's policy so you can tell your child when visits are allowed after the birth.*
- *Be sure your child knows who will be with him or her while you're in the hospital.*

MaMa Bear feels very different today. "PaPa," she says, "I think it is time for our baby to be born. We must hurry to the hospital."

PaPa calls Penny Panda, who comes right over.

MaMa kisses KoKo good-bye.

"KoKo, be a good bear for Penny. I'll be back soon," says PaPa Bear as he and MaMa leave.

KoKo and Penny wave good-bye to them.

- *Let your child help you pack your hospital bag in advance and think of things to put in it. Include a picture of him or her and a drawing to help decorate your room.*
- *Practice using the telephone with your child. This skill will be important when you are at the hospital and accessible only by phone.*
- *Have your sitter's instructions written out in advance so your departure will be smoother and more relaxed.*

Later, when PaPa Bear returns from the hospital, he has good news.

"KoKo, we have our baby! A wonderful new baby named BeBe Bear."

"Yahoo!" says KoKo.

"Shall we call MaMa at the hospital? I know she wants to talk with you," says PaPa Bear. "And let's find out when you can visit her, too."

"Yes, PaPa, let's call right now!" says KoKo.

- *Some older children show only minimal interest or even hostility towards a baby. Others are visibly delighted. Both reactions are normal and neither attitude predicts future sibling relationships.*

- *Consider hiding small presents in the house that your child can be told to "find" when you call from the hospital.*

- *Let your child help make the phone calls to announce the baby's arrival.*

That night at bedtime, KoKo asks, "PaPa, when will MaMa be home?"

"MaMa will be home soon, KoKo. It won't be long now."

"Okay, PaPa, will you read *Goldilocks and the Three Chairs?*"

"Good idea, KoKo," says PaPa Bear. "Let's get ready for bed, and then we'll read. And I need my big bear hug before you go to sleep."

- *Continuation of familiar routines is reassuring to a child whose mother is in the hospital.*
- *Place mother's picture in your child's room or ask your child to caretake something of mother's —such as a piece of jewelry—while she is gone.*
- *Before going to the hospital, tape your own readings of your child's favorite bedtime stories and books. Say "good night" at the end of each tape.*

Today MaMa and BeBe Bear are coming home.

KoKo runs to hug MaMa Bear.

"Oh, MaMa. I missed you."

"I missed you too," says MaMa, giving KoKo a big kiss.

"KoKo," says PaPa, "this is BeBe, our new bear."

"Hello, BeBe. I'm KoKo," says KoKo, standing on tiptoe to see the new baby. BeBe doesn't smile or say anything to KoKo.

- *Let someone other than mother carry the new baby when the children first meet. This helps the older child feel less displaced.*
- *Tape your child's first meeting with the new baby to preserve that moment for future replay.*
- *Let friends and relatives know that this first day you would **not** like to have drop-in visitors.*

"**K**oKo, do you want to hold BeBe?" asks MaMa Bear.

"Can I?" asks KoKo.

"Sit on the chair and we'll put BeBe on your lap. New babies don't know how to sit up. You must use your arms to help."

Holding the new bear, KoKo sees how tiny BeBe's nails are and how soft and new BeBe feels.

"Waaahh! Waaahh!"

Oh, no! BeBe Bear starts to cry. Did KoKo do something wrong?

- *Seat your child in a large couch, chair or bean-bag chair to hold the baby easily and safely.*
- *New babies can handle most "holding" positions. Your example will be the best teacher. Don't yell, "stop!" or "careful!" however much you may be tempted to.*
- *Let your child know that babies sleep and cry a lot in the beginning. Children are often surprised that a baby is not a playmate.*

"**M**aMa, BeBe is crying," says KoKo Bear.

"It's okay, KoKo. Our baby is hungry and wants to eat. Will you stay with me while I feed BeBe?" asks MaMa Bear.

"I think my Chumley is hungry, too, MaMa. Come, Chumley, stop crying. It's time to eat," says KoKo. Koko feeds Chumley from a pretend doll bottle.

- *Let your older child do as much as possible to help you with the baby. For instance, placing a step stool by the changing table allows a child to see and "help."*
- *Sitting on a couch while feeding the baby allows you to cuddle, read or watch TV with your older child.*
- *If your child invents an imaginary friend at this time, just appreciate the value of a new companion.*

T he next day the doorbell rings. It's Aunt Beartrice.

"Hi, KoKo. How are you? Where is the new baby? I have a present for BeBe Bear," she says, walking quickly past KoKo.

KoKo is surprised. *Why isn't Aunt Beartrice bringing me a present?* thinks KoKo.

- *Encourage guests to let the older sibling bring them in to see the new baby.*
- *Keep a small selection of little gifts on hand for guests who may forget to give the older child something.*
- *Don't let a child be made to feel guilty about feeling jealous. Jealousy toward a new sibling is universal. Some children feel it immediately, others several months later when the baby becomes mobile.*

"Oh, KoKo, I almost forgot. Here's YOUR present," says Aunt Beartrice.

KoKo pulls off the ribbon and wrapping paper. It's a Big Bear T-shirt!

"Thank you," says KoKo, hugging Aunt Beartrice.

Then Aunt Beartrice asks KoKo to open her present for BeBe. It's a pair of booties she knitted.

- *Explain to your child that babies "come with nothing" and need lots of things, so people give them presents.*
- *Schedule private time with your older child. Get a sitter or leave the baby with your spouse so you can do things with the child alone.*
- *Give your older child new privileges—a later bedtime or a special activity—now that he or she is a big brother or sister.*

One day KoKo peeks in to see the baby.

"Hi, BeBe. It's me. KoKo. Smile at KoKo."

BeBe's eyes open slowly and get wider and wider. Then BeBe gives KoKo a big bear smile.

"MaMa! PaPa! Come quick!" shouts KoKo. "BeBe is smiling at me. I taught BeBe how to smile," says KoKo proudly.

What would you like to teach a new baby brother or sister?

- *Keep a room intercom on in your baby's room to hear if the baby is awake or to know who else may be in there.*
- *Stress how the baby loves or enjoys having an older brother or sister.*
- *Patience, a sense of humor, and plenty of love will see you and your family through this period of adjustment.*